Cursive Handwriting

Book Adults

Children's Reading & Writing Education Books

All Rights reserved. No part of this book may be reproduced or used in any way or form or by any means whether electronic or mechanical, this means that you cannot record or photocopy any material ideas or tips that are provided in this book.

Copyright 2016

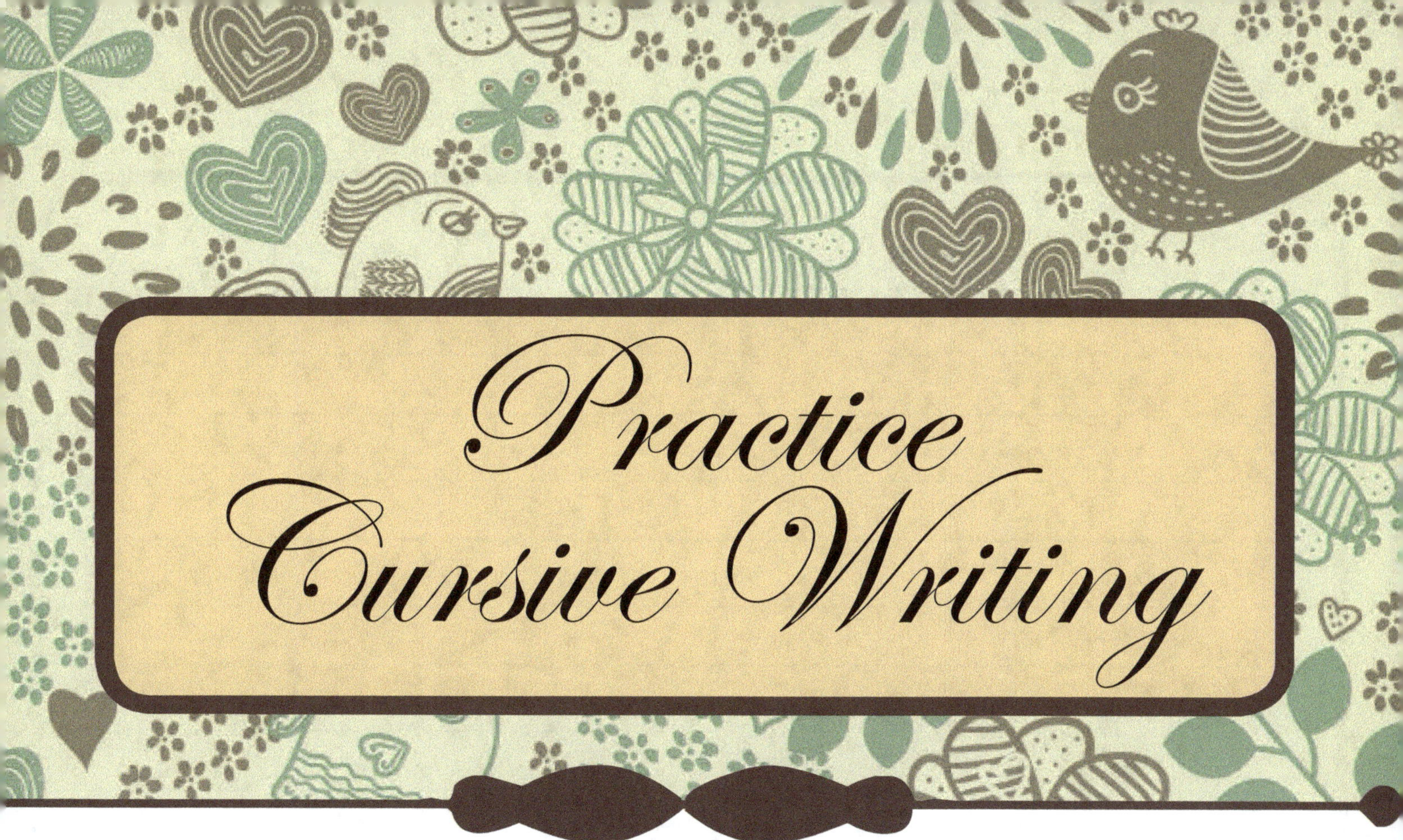

Trace and rewrite the following famous quotes.

A heart is not judged by
how much you love but by
how much you are loved by
others

— L. Frank Baum,
The Wonderful Wizard of Oz

The most beautiful things in
the world cannot be seen or
touched; they are felt with the
heart.

—Antoine de Saint-Exupéry,
The Little Prince

Why, sometimes I've believed
as many as six impossible
things before breakfast.
—Lewis Carroll,
Alice in Wonderland

We are all in the gutter, but some of us are looking at the stars.

—Oscar Wilde, Lady Windermere's Fan

I had forgotten that time
wasnt fixed like concrete but
in fact was fluid as sand, or
water. I had forgotten that
even misery can end.

—Joyce Carol Oates,
I am No One You Know

If you want to know what a mans like, take a good look at how he treats his inferiors, not his equals.

—J.K. Rowling,

Harry Potter and the Goblet of Fire

we should live like we smoke
inhale the present and exhale
the past.

—Cora Carmack,
Faking It

The richest man is not he
who has the most, but he
who needs the least.

—Unknown Author

Do not seek to follow in the footsteps of the men of old; seek what they sought.

—Basho

What we think, or what we know, or what we believe is, in the end, of little consequence. The only consequence is what we do.

— John Ruskin

No one can make you feel inferior without your consent.

—Eleanor Roosevelt,

This is My Story

What the world needs is more geniuses with humility; there are so few of us left.

—Oscar Levant

The person who reads too much and uses his brain too little will fall into lazy habits of thinking.

—Albert Einstein

We learn something every day, and lots of times its that what we learned the day before was wrong.

—Bill Vaughan

Never be afraid to laugh at yourself; after all, you could be missing out on the joke of the century.

— Dame Edna Everage

Imagination was given to
man to compensate him for
what he is not, and a sense
of humor was provided to
console him for what he is.

—Oscar Wilde

Asking a working writer what he thinks about critics is like asking a lamppost how it feels about dogs.

—Christopher Hampton

If there are no stupid questions, then what kind of questions do stupid people ask? Do they get smart just in time to ask questions?

— Scott Adams

www.ingramcontent.com/pod-product-compliance
Lightning Source LLC
LaVergne TN
LVHW082307150826
845677LV00009B/1736

9798869448873